This book belongs to:

Contact Information
Name:
Phone:
Email:

Start / End Date

\ \ to \ \

Dedication

This book is dedicated to anyone with wanderlust. Whether you travel for fun, or for work, you can make any trip worthwhile. Traveling changes you forever, and I hope this book helps you remember your trip details in a fond way.

I've traveled a lot, and each time I experience something new that gives me a fresh perspective on life. For those adventurers, those willing to brave the elements, and seek out new ways to explore our beautiful world – thank you. And enjoy the journey!

How to Use This Road Trip Travel Journal

This Road Trip Travel Journal is set up to make documenting your trip easy and fun. Writing down the information as you go along helps you remember your trip easier and stay with you longer.

I've set up this log book in the following way:

1. The first section is where you can record the Date and who you're traveling with.

2. Next you'll see a section to record the Weather Conditions.

3. The next section is where you can jot down where you're traveling to and from, the distance that will be, and how long it took.

4. Then you'll see a Traffic section to rate how bad the traffic was.

5. Next is an area to plan out your Travel Route a little more, including Stops, Time of Arrival, and Highlights/Notes. Be as detailed as possible here, and fill it out with specific moments.

6. Dining Experiences is the next section, and you can write down what you ate, how much, and what restaurants you stopped at.

7. The last section is Sleepover Experiences, where you can write your thoughts about where you're staying – the hotel, a friend's house, a camp site, etc.

All of these sections are meant to be adaptable to many types of trips, but specifically helpful for road trips.

Enjoy (and document) the journey!

DATE

TRAVELING WITH

WEATHER CONDITIONS

FROM / TO

DISTANCE

TRAVEL TIME

TRAFFIC LEVEL

LESS 1 2 3 4 5 MUCH

TRAVEL ROUTE

STOPS & MILESTONES	TIME OF ARRIVAL	HIGHLIGHTS & NOTES

DINING EXPERIENCES

BREAKFAST	LUNCH	DINNER	SNACKS

SLEEPOVER EXPERIENCES

DATE

TRAVELING WITH

WEATHER CONDITIONS

FROM / TO
DISTANCE
TRAVEL TIME

TRAFFIC LEVEL

LESS 1 2 3 4 5 MUCH

TRAVEL ROUTE

STOPS & MILESTONES	TIME OF ARRIVAL	HIGHLIGHTS & NOTES

DINING EXPERIENCES

BREAKFAST	LUNCH	DINNER	SNACKS

SLEEPOVER EXPERIENCES

Travel Log

DATE	WEATHER CONDITIONS
TRAVELING WITH	🌡 ____ ☀ ☁ 🌧 ⛈ ❄
	🚩 ____ ☐ ☐ ☐ ☐ ☐

	TRAFFIC LEVEL
FROM / TO	
DISTANCE	LESS 1 2 3 4 5 MUCH
TRAVEL TIME	○ ○ ○ ○ ○

TRAVEL ROUTE

STOPS & MILESTONES	TIME OF ARRIVAL	HIGHLIGHTS & NOTES

DINING EXPERIENCES

BREAKFAST	LUNCH	DINNER	SNACKS

SLEEPOVER EXPERIENCES

DATE		WEATHER CONDITIONS					
TRAVELING WITH		Temp: ___	☀️	⛅	🌧️	🌦️	❄️
		Wind: ___	☐	☐	☐	☐	☐

FROM / TO		TRAFFIC LEVEL
DISTANCE		LESS 1 2 3 4 5 MUCH
TRAVEL TIME		

TRAVEL ROUTE

STOPS & MILESTONES	TIME OF ARRIVAL	HIGHLIGHTS & NOTES

DINING EXPERIENCES

BREAKFAST	LUNCH	DINNER	SNACKS

SLEEPOVER EXPERIENCES

DATE	
TRAVELING WITH	

WEATHER CONDITIONS

🌡 _____ ☀ ⛅ 🌧 ⛈ ❄
🚩 _____ ☐ ☐ ☐ ☐ ☐

FROM / TO	
DISTANCE	
TRAVEL TIME	

TRAFFIC LEVEL

LESS 1 2 3 4 5 MUCH

TRAVEL ROUTE

STOPS & MILESTONES	TIME OF ARRIVAL	HIGHLIGHTS & NOTES

DINING EXPERIENCES

BREAKFAST	LUNCH	DINNER	SNACKS

SLEEPOVER EXPERIENCES

DATE

TRAVELING WITH

WEATHER CONDITIONS

☀️ ⛅ 🌧️ ⛈️ ❄️
☐ ☐ ☐ ☐ ☐

FROM / TO

DISTANCE

TRAVEL TIME

TRAFFIC LEVEL

LESS 1 2 3 4 5 MUCH
     ○ ○ ○ ○ ○

TRAVEL ROUTE

STOPS & MILESTONES	TIME OF ARRIVAL	HIGHLIGHTS & NOTES

DINING EXPERIENCES

BREAKFAST	LUNCH	DINNER	SNACKS

SLEEPOVER EXPERIENCES

DATE

TRAVELING WITH

WEATHER CONDITIONS

FROM / TO

DISTANCE

TRAVEL TIME

TRAFFIC LEVEL

LESS 1 2 3 4 5 MUCH

TRAVEL ROUTE

STOPS & MILESTONES	TIME OF ARRIVAL	HIGHLIGHTS & NOTES

DINING EXPERIENCES

BREAKFAST	LUNCH	DINNER	SNACKS

SLEEPOVER EXPERIENCES

DATE		WEATHER CONDITIONS					
TRAVELING WITH		🌡 ___	☀	⛅	🌧	⛈	❄
		🚩 ___	☐	☐	☐	☐	☐

FROM / TO		TRAFFIC LEVEL
DISTANCE		LESS 1 2 3 4 5 MUCH
TRAVEL TIME		

TRAVEL ROUTE

STOPS & MILESTONES	TIME OF ARRIVAL	HIGHLIGHTS & NOTES

DINING EXPERIENCES

BREAKFAST	LUNCH	DINNER	SNACKS

SLEEPOVER EXPERIENCES

DATE	
TRAVELING WITH	

WEATHER CONDITIONS

🌡 _____ ☀️ ⛅ 🌧 ⛈ ❄️
🌬 _____ ☐ ☐ ☐ ☐ ☐

FROM / TO	
DISTANCE	
TRAVEL TIME	

TRAFFIC LEVEL

1   2   3   4   5
○   ○   ○   ○   ○
LESS   MUCH

TRAVEL ROUTE

STOPS & MILESTONES	TIME OF ARRIVAL	HIGHLIGHTS & NOTES

DINING EXPERIENCES

BREAKFAST	LUNCH	DINNER	SNACKS

SLEEPOVER EXPERIENCES

DATE	
TRAVELING WITH	

WEATHER CONDITIONS

🌡 _____ ☀ ⛅ 🌧 ⛈ ❄
🌬 _____ ☐ ☐ ☐ ☐ ☐

FROM / TO	
DISTANCE	
TRAVEL TIME	

TRAFFIC LEVEL

LESS 1 2 3 4 5 MUCH

TRAVEL ROUTE

STOPS & MILESTONES	TIME OF ARRIVAL	HIGHLIGHTS & NOTES

DINING EXPERIENCES

BREAKFAST	LUNCH	DINNER	SNACKS

SLEEPOVER EXPERIENCES

DATE

TRAVELING WITH

WEATHER CONDITIONS

FROM / TO

DISTANCE

TRAVEL TIME

TRAFFIC LEVEL

LESS 1 — 2 — 3 — 4 — 5 MUCH

TRAVEL ROUTE

STOPS & MILESTONES	TIME OF ARRIVAL	HIGHLIGHTS & NOTES

DINING EXPERIENCES

BREAKFAST	LUNCH	DINNER	SNACKS

SLEEPOVER EXPERIENCES

DATE		WEATHER CONDITIONS
TRAVELING WITH		☀ ⛅ 🌧 ☁ ❄

FROM / TO		TRAFFIC LEVEL
DISTANCE		1 — 2 — 3 — 4 — 5
TRAVEL TIME		LESS ○ ○ ○ ○ ○ MUCH

TRAVEL ROUTE

STOPS & MILESTONES	TIME OF ARRIVAL	HIGHLIGHTS & NOTES

DINING EXPERIENCES

BREAKFAST	LUNCH	DINNER	SNACKS

SLEEPOVER EXPERIENCES

	DATE
	TRAVELING WITH

WEATHER CONDITIONS

🌡 _____   ☀ ⛅ 🌧 ⛈ ❄
🌬 _____   ☐ ☐ ☐ ☐ ☐

	FROM / TO
	DISTANCE
	TRAVEL TIME

TRAFFIC LEVEL

LESS 1 —— 2 —— 3 —— 4 —— 5 MUCH

TRAVEL ROUTE

STOPS & MILESTONES	TIME OF ARRIVAL	HIGHLIGHTS & NOTES

DINING EXPERIENCES

BREAKFAST	LUNCH	DINNER	SNACKS

SLEEPOVER EXPERIENCES

DATE

TRAVELING WITH

WEATHER CONDITIONS

FROM / TO

DISTANCE

TRAVEL TIME

TRAFFIC LEVEL

LESS 1 — 2 — 3 — 4 — 5 MUCH

TRAVEL ROUTE

STOPS & MILESTONES	TIME OF ARRIVAL	HIGHLIGHTS & NOTES

DINING EXPERIENCES

BREAKFAST	LUNCH	DINNER	SNACKS

SLEEPOVER EXPERIENCES

DATE
TRAVELING WITH

WEATHER CONDITIONS

FROM / TO
DISTANCE
TRAVEL TIME

TRAFFIC LEVEL

LESS 1 — 2 — 3 — 4 — 5 MUCH

TRAVEL ROUTE

STOPS & MILESTONES	TIME OF ARRIVAL	HIGHLIGHTS & NOTES

DINING EXPERIENCES

BREAKFAST	LUNCH	DINNER	SNACKS

SLEEPOVER EXPERIENCES

DATE

TRAVELING WITH

WEATHER CONDITIONS

FROM / TO

DISTANCE

TRAVEL TIME

TRAFFIC LEVEL

LESS 1 — 2 — 3 — 4 — 5 MUCH

TRAVEL ROUTE

STOPS & MILESTONES	TIME OF ARRIVAL	HIGHLIGHTS & NOTES

DINING EXPERIENCES

BREAKFAST	LUNCH	DINNER	SNACKS

SLEEPOVER EXPERIENCES

DATE

TRAVELING WITH

WEATHER CONDITIONS

🌡 _____ ☀ ⛅ 🌧 ⛈ ❄
💨 _____ ☐ ☐ ☐ ☐ ☐

FROM / TO

DISTANCE

TRAVEL TIME

TRAFFIC LEVEL

LESS 1 2 3 4 5 MUCH

TRAVEL ROUTE

STOPS & MILESTONES	TIME OF ARRIVAL	HIGHLIGHTS & NOTES

DINING EXPERIENCES

BREAKFAST	LUNCH	DINNER	SNACKS

SLEEPOVER EXPERIENCES

DATE

TRAVELING WITH

WEATHER CONDITIONS

FROM / TO
DISTANCE
TRAVEL TIME

TRAFFIC LEVEL

LESS 1 2 3 4 5 MUCH

TRAVEL ROUTE

STOPS & MILESTONES	TIME OF ARRIVAL	HIGHLIGHTS & NOTES

DINING EXPERIENCES

BREAKFAST	LUNCH	DINNER	SNACKS

SLEEPOVER EXPERIENCES

DATE

TRAVELING WITH

WEATHER CONDITIONS

☀️ ☁️ 🌧️ ⛈️ ❄️
☐ ☐ ☐ ☐ ☐

FROM / TO

DISTANCE

TRAVEL TIME

TRAFFIC LEVEL

LESS 1 2 3 4 5 MUCH

TRAVEL ROUTE

STOPS & MILESTONES	TIME OF ARRIVAL	HIGHLIGHTS & NOTES

DINING EXPERIENCES

BREAKFAST	LUNCH	DINNER	SNACKS

SLEEPOVER EXPERIENCES

DATE

TRAVELING WITH

WEATHER CONDITIONS

FROM / TO

DISTANCE

TRAVEL TIME

TRAFFIC LEVEL

LESS 1 2 3 4 5 MUCH

TRAVEL ROUTE

STOPS & MILESTONES	TIME OF ARRIVAL	HIGHLIGHTS & NOTES

DINING EXPERIENCES

BREAKFAST	LUNCH	DINNER	SNACKS

SLEEPOVER EXPERIENCES

DATE		WEATHER CONDITIONS
TRAVELING WITH		

		TRAFFIC LEVEL
FROM / TO		
DISTANCE		LESS 1 2 3 4 5 MUCH
TRAVEL TIME		

TRAVEL ROUTE

STOPS & MILESTONES	TIME OF ARRIVAL	HIGHLIGHTS & NOTES

DINING EXPERIENCES

BREAKFAST	LUNCH	DINNER	SNACKS

SLEEPOVER EXPERIENCES

DATE	
TRAVELING WITH	

WEATHER CONDITIONS

🌡 _____ ☀ ⛅ 🌧 ⛈ ❄
🚩 _____ ☐ ☐ ☐ ☐ ☐

FROM / TO	
DISTANCE	
TRAVEL TIME	

TRAFFIC LEVEL

LESS 1 — 2 — 3 — 4 — 5 MUCH

TRAVEL ROUTE

STOPS & MILESTONES	TIME OF ARRIVAL	HIGHLIGHTS & NOTES

DINING EXPERIENCES

BREAKFAST	LUNCH	DINNER	SNACKS

SLEEPOVER EXPERIENCES

DATE	WEATHER CONDITIONS
TRAVELING WITH	☀️ ⛅ 🌧️ ⛈️ ❄️
	☐ ☐ ☐ ☐ ☐

FROM / TO	TRAFFIC LEVEL
DISTANCE	LESS 1 2 3 4 5 MUCH
TRAVEL TIME	○ ○ ○ ○ ○

TRAVEL ROUTE

STOPS & MILESTONES	TIME OF ARRIVAL	HIGHLIGHTS & NOTES

DINING EXPERIENCES

BREAKFAST	LUNCH	DINNER	SNACKS

SLEEPOVER EXPERIENCES

DATE

TRAVELING WITH

WEATHER CONDITIONS

FROM / TO

DISTANCE

TRAVEL TIME

TRAFFIC LEVEL

LESS 1 2 3 4 5 MUCH

TRAVEL ROUTE

STOPS & MILESTONES	TIME OF ARRIVAL	HIGHLIGHTS & NOTES

DINING EXPERIENCES

BREAKFAST	LUNCH	DINNER	SNACKS

SLEEPOVER EXPERIENCES

DATE		WEATHER CONDITIONS
TRAVELING WITH		🌡 ____ ☀ ⛅ 🌧 ⛈ ❄
		🚩 ____ ☐ ☐ ☐ ☐ ☐

FROM / TO		TRAFFIC LEVEL
DISTANCE		LESS 1 2 3 4 5 MUCH
TRAVEL TIME		○ ○ ○ ○ ○

TRAVEL ROUTE

STOPS & MILESTONES	TIME OF ARRIVAL	HIGHLIGHTS & NOTES

DINING EXPERIENCES

BREAKFAST	LUNCH	DINNER	SNACKS

SLEEPOVER EXPERIENCES

DATE	WEATHER CONDITIONS
TRAVELING WITH	🌡 ___ ☀ ⛅ 🌧 ⛈ ❄
	🎐 ___ ☐ ☐ ☐ ☐ ☐

FROM / TO	TRAFFIC LEVEL
DISTANCE	LESS 1 2 3 4 5 MUCH
TRAVEL TIME	

TRAVEL ROUTE

STOPS & MILESTONES	TIME OF ARRIVAL	HIGHLIGHTS & NOTES

DINING EXPERIENCES

BREAKFAST	LUNCH	DINNER	SNACKS

SLEEPOVER EXPERIENCES

Travel Log

DATE	
TRAVELING WITH	

WEATHER CONDITIONS

🌡️ ___	☀️	⛅	🌧️	⛈️	❄️
🚩 ___	☐	☐	☐	☐	☐

FROM / TO	
DISTANCE	
TRAVEL TIME	

TRAFFIC LEVEL

LESS 1 ○ 2 ○ 3 ○ 4 ○ 5 ○ MUCH

TRAVEL ROUTE

STOPS & MILESTONES	TIME OF ARRIVAL	HIGHLIGHTS & NOTES

DINING EXPERIENCES

BREAKFAST	LUNCH	DINNER	SNACKS

SLEEPOVER EXPERIENCES

DATE	
TRAVELING WITH	

WEATHER CONDITIONS

🌡 _____ ☀ ⛅ 🌧 ⛈ ❄
🚩 _____ ☐ ☐ ☐ ☐ ☐

FROM / TO	
DISTANCE	
TRAVEL TIME	

TRAFFIC LEVEL

LESS 1 2 3 4 5 MUCH

TRAVEL ROUTE

STOPS & MILESTONES	TIME OF ARRIVAL	HIGHLIGHTS & NOTES

DINING EXPERIENCES

BREAKFAST	LUNCH	DINNER	SNACKS

SLEEPOVER EXPERIENCES

	DATE
	TRAVELING WITH

WEATHER CONDITIONS

🌡 _____ ☀ ⛅ 🌧 ⛈ ❄
🌬 _____ ☐ ☐ ☐ ☐ ☐

	FROM / TO
	DISTANCE
	TRAVEL TIME

TRAFFIC LEVEL

LESS 1 — 2 — 3 — 4 — 5 MUCH

TRAVEL ROUTE

STOPS & MILESTONES	TIME OF ARRIVAL	HIGHLIGHTS & NOTES

DINING EXPERIENCES

BREAKFAST	LUNCH	DINNER	SNACKS

SLEEPOVER EXPERIENCES

_____
_____
_____

DATE

TRAVELING WITH

WEATHER CONDITIONS

FROM / TO
DISTANCE
TRAVEL TIME

TRAFFIC LEVEL

LESS 1 2 3 4 5 MUCH

TRAVEL ROUTE

STOPS & MILESTONES	TIME OF ARRIVAL	HIGHLIGHTS & NOTES

DINING EXPERIENCES

BREAKFAST	LUNCH	DINNER	SNACKS

SLEEPOVER EXPERIENCES

DATE

TRAVELING WITH

WEATHER CONDITIONS

FROM / TO

DISTANCE

TRAVEL TIME

TRAFFIC LEVEL

LESS 1 2 3 4 5 MUCH

TRAVEL ROUTE

STOPS & MILESTONES	TIME OF ARRIVAL	HIGHLIGHTS & NOTES

DINING EXPERIENCES

BREAKFAST	LUNCH	DINNER	SNACKS

SLEEPOVER EXPERIENCES

DATE

TRAVELING WITH

WEATHER CONDITIONS

☀ ⛅ 🌧 ⛈ ❄
☐ ☐ ☐ ☐ ☐

FROM / TO

DISTANCE

TRAVEL TIME

TRAFFIC LEVEL

LESS 1 2 3 4 5 MUCH

TRAVEL ROUTE

STOPS & MILESTONES	TIME OF ARRIVAL	HIGHLIGHTS & NOTES

DINING EXPERIENCES

BREAKFAST	LUNCH	DINNER	SNACKS

SLEEPOVER EXPERIENCES

	DATE
	TRAVELING WITH

WEATHER CONDITIONS

🌡 _____ ☀️ ⛅ 🌧 ⛈ ❄️
🪁 _____ ☐ ☐ ☐ ☐ ☐

	FROM / TO
	DISTANCE
	TRAVEL TIME

TRAFFIC LEVEL

LESS 1 — 2 — 3 — 4 — 5 MUCH

TRAVEL ROUTE

STOPS & MILESTONES	TIME OF ARRIVAL	HIGHLIGHTS & NOTES

DINING EXPERIENCES

BREAKFAST	LUNCH	DINNER	SNACKS

SLEEPOVER EXPERIENCES

DATE		WEATHER CONDITIONS
TRAVELING WITH		☀️ ⛅ 🌧️ ⛈️ ❄️
		☐ ☐ ☐ ☐ ☐

FROM / TO		TRAFFIC LEVEL
DISTANCE		LESS 1 — 2 — 3 — 4 — 5 MUCH
TRAVEL TIME		

TRAVEL ROUTE

STOPS & MILESTONES	TIME OF ARRIVAL	HIGHLIGHTS & NOTES

DINING EXPERIENCES

BREAKFAST	LUNCH	DINNER	SNACKS

SLEEPOVER EXPERIENCES

DATE	
TRAVELING WITH	

WEATHER CONDITIONS

🌡 _____ ☀ ⛅ 🌧 ⛈ ❄
💨 _____ ☐ ☐ ☐ ☐ ☐

FROM / TO	
DISTANCE	
TRAVEL TIME	

TRAFFIC LEVEL

LESS 1 2 3 4 5 MUCH

TRAVEL ROUTE

STOPS & MILESTONES	TIME OF ARRIVAL	HIGHLIGHTS & NOTES

DINING EXPERIENCES

BREAKFAST	LUNCH	DINNER	SNACKS

SLEEPOVER EXPERIENCES

DATE

TRAVELING WITH

WEATHER CONDITIONS

FROM / TO

DISTANCE

TRAVEL TIME

TRAFFIC LEVEL

LESS 1 2 3 4 5 MUCH

TRAVEL ROUTE

STOPS & MILESTONES	TIME OF ARRIVAL	HIGHLIGHTS & NOTES

DINING EXPERIENCES

BREAKFAST	LUNCH	DINNER	SNACKS

SLEEPOVER EXPERIENCES

	DATE
	TRAVELING WITH

WEATHER CONDITIONS

🌡 _____ ☀ ⛅ 🌧 ⛈ ❄
🌬 _____ ☐ ☐ ☐ ☐ ☐

	FROM / TO
	DISTANCE
	TRAVEL TIME

TRAFFIC LEVEL

LESS 1 2 3 4 5 MUCH

TRAVEL ROUTE

STOPS & MILESTONES	TIME OF ARRIVAL	HIGHLIGHTS & NOTES

DINING EXPERIENCES

BREAKFAST	LUNCH	DINNER	SNACKS

SLEEPOVER EXPERIENCES

DATE		WEATHER CONDITIONS	
TRAVELING WITH		☀️ ⛅ 🌧️ ⛈️ ❄️	

FROM / TO		TRAFFIC LEVEL	
DISTANCE		LESS 1 2 3 4 5 MUCH	
TRAVEL TIME			

TRAVEL ROUTE

STOPS & MILESTONES	TIME OF ARRIVAL	HIGHLIGHTS & NOTES

DINING EXPERIENCES

BREAKFAST	LUNCH	DINNER	SNACKS

SLEEPOVER EXPERIENCES

DATE

TRAVELING WITH

WEATHER CONDITIONS

FROM / TO

DISTANCE

TRAVEL TIME

TRAFFIC LEVEL

LESS 1 — 2 — 3 — 4 — 5 MUCH

TRAVEL ROUTE

STOPS & MILESTONES	TIME OF ARRIVAL	HIGHLIGHTS & NOTES

DINING EXPERIENCES

BREAKFAST	LUNCH	DINNER	SNACKS

SLEEPOVER EXPERIENCES

DATE	
TRAVELING WITH	

WEATHER CONDITIONS

🌡 _____ ☀ ⛅ 🌧 ⛈ ❄
🏴 _____ ☐ ☐ ☐ ☐ ☐

FROM / TO	
DISTANCE	
TRAVEL TIME	

TRAFFIC LEVEL

LESS 1 2 3 4 5 MUCH

TRAVEL ROUTE

STOPS & MILESTONES	TIME OF ARRIVAL	HIGHLIGHTS & NOTES

DINING EXPERIENCES

BREAKFAST	LUNCH	DINNER	SNACKS

SLEEPOVER EXPERIENCES

DATE	
TRAVELING WITH	

WEATHER CONDITIONS

🌡 _____ ☀ ⛅ 🌦 ⛈ ❄
🌬 _____ ☐ ☐ ☐ ☐ ☐

FROM / TO	
DISTANCE	
TRAVEL TIME	

TRAFFIC LEVEL

LESS 1 — 2 — 3 — 4 — 5 MUCH

TRAVEL ROUTE

STOPS & MILESTONES	TIME OF ARRIVAL	HIGHLIGHTS & NOTES

DINING EXPERIENCES

BREAKFAST	LUNCH	DINNER	SNACKS

SLEEPOVER EXPERIENCES

DATE

TRAVELING WITH

WEATHER CONDITIONS

FROM / TO

DISTANCE

TRAVEL TIME

TRAFFIC LEVEL

LESS 1 2 3 4 5 MUCH

TRAVEL ROUTE

STOPS & MILESTONES	TIME OF ARRIVAL	HIGHLIGHTS & NOTES

DINING EXPERIENCES

BREAKFAST	LUNCH	DINNER	SNACKS

SLEEPOVER EXPERIENCES

DATE	
TRAVELING WITH	

WEATHER CONDITIONS

🌡 ____ ☀️ ⛅ 🌧 ⛈ ❄️

🚩 ____ ☐ ☐ ☐ ☐ ☐

FROM / TO	
DISTANCE	
TRAVEL TIME	

TRAFFIC LEVEL

LESS 1 — 2 — 3 — 4 — 5 MUCH

TRAVEL ROUTE

STOPS & MILESTONES	TIME OF ARRIVAL	HIGHLIGHTS & NOTES

DINING EXPERIENCES

BREAKFAST	LUNCH	DINNER	SNACKS

SLEEPOVER EXPERIENCES

DATE		WEATHER CONDITIONS
TRAVELING WITH		☀ ⛅ 🌧 ⛈ ❄

FROM / TO		TRAFFIC LEVEL
DISTANCE		1 2 3 4 5
TRAVEL TIME		LESS ——————— MUCH

TRAVEL ROUTE

STOPS & MILESTONES	TIME OF ARRIVAL	HIGHLIGHTS & NOTES

DINING EXPERIENCES

BREAKFAST	LUNCH	DINNER	SNACKS

SLEEPOVER EXPERIENCES

DATE	
TRAVELING WITH	

WEATHER CONDITIONS

🌡 _____   ☀ ⛅ 🌧 ⛈ ❄
🎐 _____   ☐ ☐ ☐ ☐ ☐

FROM / TO	
DISTANCE	
TRAVEL TIME	

TRAFFIC LEVEL

LESS 1 — 2 — 3 — 4 — 5 MUCH

TRAVEL ROUTE

STOPS & MILESTONES	TIME OF ARRIVAL	HIGHLIGHTS & NOTES

DINING EXPERIENCES

BREAKFAST	LUNCH	DINNER	SNACKS

SLEEPOVER EXPERIENCES

DATE

TRAVELING WITH

WEATHER CONDITIONS

FROM / TO

DISTANCE

TRAVEL TIME

TRAFFIC LEVEL

LESS 1 — 2 — 3 — 4 — 5 MUCH

TRAVEL ROUTE

STOPS & MILESTONES	TIME OF ARRIVAL	HIGHLIGHTS & NOTES

DINING EXPERIENCES

BREAKFAST	LUNCH	DINNER	SNACKS

SLEEPOVER EXPERIENCES

DATE

TRAVELING WITH

WEATHER CONDITIONS

FROM / TO

DISTANCE

TRAVEL TIME

TRAFFIC LEVEL

LESS 1 2 3 4 5 MUCH

TRAVEL ROUTE

STOPS & MILESTONES	TIME OF ARRIVAL	HIGHLIGHTS & NOTES

DINING EXPERIENCES

BREAKFAST	LUNCH	DINNER	SNACKS

SLEEPOVER EXPERIENCES

DATE		WEATHER CONDITIONS

TRAVELING WITH

FROM / TO		TRAFFIC LEVEL
DISTANCE		LESS 1 2 3 4 5 MUCH
TRAVEL TIME		

TRAVEL ROUTE

STOPS & MILESTONES	TIME OF ARRIVAL	HIGHLIGHTS & NOTES

DINING EXPERIENCES

BREAKFAST	LUNCH	DINNER	SNACKS

SLEEPOVER EXPERIENCES

DATE	
TRAVELING WITH	

WEATHER CONDITIONS

🌡️ _____ ☀️ ⛅ 🌧️ ⛈️ ❄️
💨 _____ ☐ ☐ ☐ ☐ ☐

FROM / TO	
DISTANCE	
TRAVEL TIME	

TRAFFIC LEVEL

LESS 1 — 2 — 3 — 4 — 5 MUCH

TRAVEL ROUTE

STOPS & MILESTONES	TIME OF ARRIVAL	HIGHLIGHTS & NOTES

DINING EXPERIENCES

BREAKFAST	LUNCH	DINNER	SNACKS

SLEEPOVER EXPERIENCES

DATE	
TRAVELING WITH	

WEATHER CONDITIONS

🌡 _____ ☀️ 🌤 🌧 ⛈ ❄️
🚩 _____ ☐ ☐ ☐ ☐ ☐

FROM / TO	
DISTANCE	
TRAVEL TIME	

TRAFFIC LEVEL

LESS 1 2 3 4 5 MUCH

TRAVEL ROUTE

STOPS & MILESTONES	TIME OF ARRIVAL	HIGHLIGHTS & NOTES

DINING EXPERIENCES

BREAKFAST	LUNCH	DINNER	SNACKS

SLEEPOVER EXPERIENCES

DATE

TRAVELING WITH

WEATHER CONDITIONS

☀️ ⛅ 🌧️ ⛈️ ❄️
☐ ☐ ☐ ☐ ☐

FROM / TO

DISTANCE

TRAVEL TIME

TRAFFIC LEVEL

LESS 1 — 2 — 3 — 4 — 5 MUCH
○ ○ ○ ○ ○

TRAVEL ROUTE

STOPS & MILESTONES	TIME OF ARRIVAL	HIGHLIGHTS & NOTES

DINING EXPERIENCES

BREAKFAST	LUNCH	DINNER	SNACKS

SLEEPOVER EXPERIENCES

DATE

TRAVELING WITH

WEATHER CONDITIONS

FROM / TO
DISTANCE
TRAVEL TIME

TRAFFIC LEVEL

LESS 1 2 3 4 5 MUCH

TRAVEL ROUTE

STOPS & MILESTONES	TIME OF ARRIVAL	HIGHLIGHTS & NOTES

DINING EXPERIENCES

BREAKFAST	LUNCH	DINNER	SNACKS

SLEEPOVER EXPERIENCES

DATE

TRAVELING WITH

WEATHER CONDITIONS

🌡 _____ ☀ ⛅ 🌧 ⛈ ❄
🚩 _____ ☐ ☐ ☐ ☐ ☐

FROM / TO

DISTANCE

TRAVEL TIME

TRAFFIC LEVEL

LESS 1 2 3 4 5 MUCH
      ○ ○ ○ ○ ○

TRAVEL ROUTE

STOPS & MILESTONES	TIME OF ARRIVAL	HIGHLIGHTS & NOTES

DINING EXPERIENCES

BREAKFAST	LUNCH	DINNER	SNACKS

SLEEPOVER EXPERIENCES

DATE

TRAVELING WITH

WEATHER CONDITIONS

☀️ ⛅ 🌧️ ⛈️ ❄️
☐ ☐ ☐ ☐ ☐

FROM / TO

DISTANCE

TRAVEL TIME

TRAFFIC LEVEL

LESS 1 — 2 — 3 — 4 — 5 MUCH

TRAVEL ROUTE

STOPS & MILESTONES	TIME OF ARRIVAL	HIGHLIGHTS & NOTES

DINING EXPERIENCES

BREAKFAST	LUNCH	DINNER	SNACKS

SLEEPOVER EXPERIENCES

	DATE
	TRAVELING WITH

WEATHER CONDITIONS					
🌡 ___	☀	⛅	🌧	⛈	❄
🚩 ___	☐	☐	☐	☐	☐

	FROM / TO
	DISTANCE
	TRAVEL TIME

TRAFFIC LEVEL

LESS 1 — 2 — 3 — 4 — 5 MUCH

TRAVEL ROUTE

STOPS & MILESTONES	TIME OF ARRIVAL	HIGHLIGHTS & NOTES

DINING EXPERIENCES

BREAKFAST	LUNCH	DINNER	SNACKS

SLEEPOVER EXPERIENCES

DATE

TRAVELING WITH

WEATHER CONDITIONS

☀ ⛅ 🌧 ⛈ ❄
☐ ☐ ☐ ☐ ☐

FROM / TO

DISTANCE

TRAVEL TIME

TRAFFIC LEVEL

LESS 1 2 3 4 5 MUCH

TRAVEL ROUTE

STOPS & MILESTONES	TIME OF ARRIVAL	HIGHLIGHTS & NOTES

DINING EXPERIENCES

BREAKFAST	LUNCH	DINNER	SNACKS

SLEEPOVER EXPERIENCES

DATE		WEATHER CONDITIONS	
TRAVELING WITH		☀️ ⛅ 🌧️ ⛈️ ❄️	

FROM / TO		TRAFFIC LEVEL	
DISTANCE		LESS 1 — 2 — 3 — 4 — 5 MUCH	
TRAVEL TIME			

TRAVEL ROUTE

STOPS & MILESTONES	TIME OF ARRIVAL	HIGHLIGHTS & NOTES

DINING EXPERIENCES

BREAKFAST	LUNCH	DINNER	SNACKS

SLEEPOVER EXPERIENCES

DATE
TRAVELING WITH

WEATHER CONDITIONS

FROM / TO
DISTANCE
TRAVEL TIME

TRAFFIC LEVEL

LESS 1 2 3 4 5 MUCH

TRAVEL ROUTE

STOPS & MILESTONES	TIME OF ARRIVAL	HIGHLIGHTS & NOTES

DINING EXPERIENCES

BREAKFAST	LUNCH	DINNER	SNACKS

SLEEPOVER EXPERIENCES

DATE		WEATHER CONDITIONS					
TRAVELING WITH		🌡 ___	☀	⛅	🌧	⛈	❄
		🎐 ___	☐	☐	☐	☐	☐

FROM / TO
DISTANCE
TRAVEL TIME

TRAFFIC LEVEL
LESS 1 — 2 — 3 — 4 — 5 MUCH

TRAVEL ROUTE

STOPS & MILESTONES	TIME OF ARRIVAL	HIGHLIGHTS & NOTES

DINING EXPERIENCES

BREAKFAST	LUNCH	DINNER	SNACKS

SLEEPOVER EXPERIENCES

DATE

TRAVELING WITH

WEATHER CONDITIONS

☀ ⛅ 🌧 ⛈ ❄
☐ ☐ ☐ ☐ ☐

FROM / TO

DISTANCE

TRAVEL TIME

TRAFFIC LEVEL

LESS 1 2 3 4 5 MUCH

TRAVEL ROUTE

STOPS & MILESTONES	TIME OF ARRIVAL	HIGHLIGHTS & NOTES

DINING EXPERIENCES

BREAKFAST	LUNCH	DINNER	SNACKS

SLEEPOVER EXPERIENCES

DATE

TRAVELING WITH

WEATHER CONDITIONS

☀️ ⛅ 🌧️ ⛈️ ❄️
☐ ☐ ☐ ☐ ☐

FROM / TO

DISTANCE

TRAVEL TIME

TRAFFIC LEVEL

LESS 1 — 2 — 3 — 4 — 5 MUCH
○ ○ ○ ○ ○

TRAVEL ROUTE

STOPS & MILESTONES	TIME OF ARRIVAL	HIGHLIGHTS & NOTES

DINING EXPERIENCES

BREAKFAST	LUNCH	DINNER	SNACKS

SLEEPOVER EXPERIENCES

DATE

TRAVELING WITH

WEATHER CONDITIONS

FROM / TO

DISTANCE

TRAVEL TIME

TRAFFIC LEVEL

LESS 1 2 3 4 5 MUCH

TRAVEL ROUTE

STOPS & MILESTONES	TIME OF ARRIVAL	HIGHLIGHTS & NOTES

DINING EXPERIENCES

BREAKFAST	LUNCH	DINNER	SNACKS

SLEEPOVER EXPERIENCES

DATE	
TRAVELING WITH	

WEATHER CONDITIONS

🌡 ____ ☀ ⛅ 🌧 ⛈ ❄
🪁 ____ ☐ ☐ ☐ ☐ ☐

FROM / TO	
DISTANCE	
TRAVEL TIME	

TRAFFIC LEVEL

LESS 1 2 3 4 5 MUCH

TRAVEL ROUTE

STOPS & MILESTONES	TIME OF ARRIVAL	HIGHLIGHTS & NOTES

DINING EXPERIENCES

BREAKFAST	LUNCH	DINNER	SNACKS

SLEEPOVER EXPERIENCES

DATE

TRAVELING WITH

WEATHER CONDITIONS

☀️ ⛅ 🌧️ ⛈️ ❄️
☐ ☐ ☐ ☐ ☐

FROM / TO

DISTANCE

TRAVEL TIME

TRAFFIC LEVEL

LESS 1 2 3 4 5 MUCH

TRAVEL ROUTE

STOPS & MILESTONES	TIME OF ARRIVAL	HIGHLIGHTS & NOTES

DINING EXPERIENCES

BREAKFAST	LUNCH	DINNER	SNACKS

SLEEPOVER EXPERIENCES

DATE		WEATHER CONDITIONS	
TRAVELING WITH		🌡 ____ ☀ ⛅ 🌧 ⛈ ❄	
		🚩 ____ ☐ ☐ ☐ ☐ ☐	

FROM / TO		TRAFFIC LEVEL
DISTANCE		LESS 1 2 3 4 5 MUCH
TRAVEL TIME		○ ○ ○ ○ ○

TRAVEL ROUTE

STOPS & MILESTONES	TIME OF ARRIVAL	HIGHLIGHTS & NOTES

DINING EXPERIENCES

BREAKFAST	LUNCH	DINNER	SNACKS

SLEEPOVER EXPERIENCES

DATE

TRAVELING WITH

WEATHER CONDITIONS

☀️ ⛅ 🌧️ ⛈️ ❄️
☐ ☐ ☐ ☐ ☐

FROM / TO

DISTANCE

TRAVEL TIME

TRAFFIC LEVEL

LESS 1 — 2 — 3 — 4 — 5 MUCH

TRAVEL ROUTE

STOPS & MILESTONES	TIME OF ARRIVAL	HIGHLIGHTS & NOTES

DINING EXPERIENCES

BREAKFAST	LUNCH	DINNER	SNACKS

SLEEPOVER EXPERIENCES

DATE

TRAVELING WITH

WEATHER CONDITIONS

FROM / TO

DISTANCE

TRAVEL TIME

TRAFFIC LEVEL

LESS 1 2 3 4 5 MUCH

TRAVEL ROUTE

STOPS & MILESTONES	TIME OF ARRIVAL	HIGHLIGHTS & NOTES

DINING EXPERIENCES

BREAKFAST	LUNCH	DINNER	SNACKS

SLEEPOVER EXPERIENCES

📅 DATE	
🎒 TRAVELING WITH	

WEATHER CONDITIONS

🌡 _____ ☀️ ⛅ 🌦 🌧 ❄️
🎐 _____ ☐ ☐ ☐ ☐ ☐

🗺 FROM / TO	
📍 DISTANCE	
🕐 TRAVEL TIME	

TRAFFIC LEVEL

LESS 1 2 3 4 5 MUCH
       ○ ○ ○ ○ ○

TRAVEL ROUTE

STOPS & MILESTONES	TIME OF ARRIVAL	HIGHLIGHTS & NOTES

DINING EXPERIENCES

BREAKFAST	LUNCH	DINNER	SNACKS

SLEEPOVER EXPERIENCES

DATE		WEATHER CONDITIONS					
TRAVELING WITH		🌡 ___	☀	⛅	🌧	⛈	❄
		🎐 ___	☐	☐	☐	☐	☐

FROM / TO
DISTANCE
TRAVEL TIME

TRAFFIC LEVEL
LESS 1 — 2 — 3 — 4 — 5 MUCH

TRAVEL ROUTE

STOPS & MILESTONES	TIME OF ARRIVAL	HIGHLIGHTS & NOTES

DINING EXPERIENCES

BREAKFAST	LUNCH	DINNER	SNACKS

SLEEPOVER EXPERIENCES

DATE	
TRAVELING WITH	

WEATHER CONDITIONS

🌡 _____ ☀ ⛅ 🌧 ⛈ ❄
🚩 _____ ☐ ☐ ☐ ☐ ☐

FROM / TO	
DISTANCE	
TRAVEL TIME	

TRAFFIC LEVEL

LESS 1 — 2 — 3 — 4 — 5 MUCH

TRAVEL ROUTE

STOPS & MILESTONES	TIME OF ARRIVAL	HIGHLIGHTS & NOTES

DINING EXPERIENCES

BREAKFAST	LUNCH	DINNER	SNACKS

SLEEPOVER EXPERIENCES

DATE

TRAVELING WITH

WEATHER CONDITIONS

FROM / TO

DISTANCE

TRAVEL TIME

TRAFFIC LEVEL

LESS 1 2 3 4 5 MUCH

TRAVEL ROUTE

STOPS & MILESTONES	TIME OF ARRIVAL	HIGHLIGHTS & NOTES

DINING EXPERIENCES

BREAKFAST	LUNCH	DINNER	SNACKS

SLEEPOVER EXPERIENCES

DATE

TRAVELING WITH

WEATHER CONDITIONS

FROM / TO

DISTANCE

TRAVEL TIME

TRAFFIC LEVEL

LESS 1 — 2 — 3 — 4 — 5 MUCH

TRAVEL ROUTE

STOPS & MILESTONES	TIME OF ARRIVAL	HIGHLIGHTS & NOTES

DINING EXPERIENCES

BREAKFAST	LUNCH	DINNER	SNACKS

SLEEPOVER EXPERIENCES

DATE	
TRAVELING WITH	

WEATHER CONDITIONS

🌡 _____ ☀ ⛅ 🌧 ⛈ ❄
🌬 _____ ☐ ☐ ☐ ☐ ☐

FROM / TO	
DISTANCE	
TRAVEL TIME	

TRAFFIC LEVEL

LESS 1 2 3 4 5 MUCH

TRAVEL ROUTE

STOPS & MILESTONES	TIME OF ARRIVAL	HIGHLIGHTS & NOTES

DINING EXPERIENCES

BREAKFAST	LUNCH	DINNER	SNACKS

SLEEPOVER EXPERIENCES

DATE

TRAVELING WITH

WEATHER CONDITIONS

FROM / TO

DISTANCE

TRAVEL TIME

TRAFFIC LEVEL

LESS 1 — 2 — 3 — 4 — 5 MUCH

TRAVEL ROUTE

STOPS & MILESTONES	TIME OF ARRIVAL	HIGHLIGHTS & NOTES

DINING EXPERIENCES

BREAKFAST	LUNCH	DINNER	SNACKS

SLEEPOVER EXPERIENCES

DATE

TRAVELING WITH

WEATHER CONDITIONS

☀️ ⛅ 🌧️ ⛈️ ❄️
☐ ☐ ☐ ☐ ☐

FROM / TO

DISTANCE

TRAVEL TIME

TRAFFIC LEVEL

LESS 1 2 3 4 5 MUCH

TRAVEL ROUTE

STOPS & MILESTONES	TIME OF ARRIVAL	HIGHLIGHTS & NOTES

DINING EXPERIENCES

BREAKFAST	LUNCH	DINNER	SNACKS

SLEEPOVER EXPERIENCES

DATE

TRAVELING WITH

WEATHER CONDITIONS

☀️ ⛅ 🌧️ ⛈️ ❄️
☐ ☐ ☐ ☐ ☐

FROM / TO

DISTANCE

TRAVEL TIME

TRAFFIC LEVEL

LESS 1 2 3 4 5 MUCH

TRAVEL ROUTE

STOPS & MILESTONES	TIME OF ARRIVAL	HIGHLIGHTS & NOTES

DINING EXPERIENCES

BREAKFAST	LUNCH	DINNER	SNACKS

SLEEPOVER EXPERIENCES

DATE	
TRAVELING WITH	

WEATHER CONDITIONS

🌡️ _____ ☀️ ⛅ 🌧️ ⛈️ ❄️
🚩 _____ ☐ ☐ ☐ ☐ ☐

FROM / TO	
DISTANCE	
TRAVEL TIME	

TRAFFIC LEVEL

LESS 1 — 2 — 3 — 4 — 5 MUCH

TRAVEL ROUTE

STOPS & MILESTONES	TIME OF ARRIVAL	HIGHLIGHTS & NOTES

DINING EXPERIENCES

BREAKFAST	LUNCH	DINNER	SNACKS

SLEEPOVER EXPERIENCES

DATE

TRAVELING WITH

WEATHER CONDITIONS

FROM / TO

DISTANCE

TRAVEL TIME

TRAFFIC LEVEL

LESS 1 2 3 4 5 MUCH

TRAVEL ROUTE

STOPS & MILESTONES	TIME OF ARRIVAL	HIGHLIGHTS & NOTES

DINING EXPERIENCES

BREAKFAST	LUNCH	DINNER	SNACKS

SLEEPOVER EXPERIENCES

DATE		WEATHER CONDITIONS	
TRAVELING WITH		☀ ⛅ 🌧 ⛈ ❄	

FROM / TO		TRAFFIC LEVEL
DISTANCE		LESS 1 — 2 — 3 — 4 — 5 MUCH
TRAVEL TIME		

TRAVEL ROUTE

STOPS & MILESTONES	TIME OF ARRIVAL	HIGHLIGHTS & NOTES

DINING EXPERIENCES

BREAKFAST	LUNCH	DINNER	SNACKS

SLEEPOVER EXPERIENCES

DATE

TRAVELING WITH

WEATHER CONDITIONS

FROM / TO

DISTANCE

TRAVEL TIME

TRAFFIC LEVEL

LESS 1 2 3 4 5 MUCH

TRAVEL ROUTE

STOPS & MILESTONES	TIME OF ARRIVAL	HIGHLIGHTS & NOTES

DINING EXPERIENCES

BREAKFAST	LUNCH	DINNER	SNACKS

SLEEPOVER EXPERIENCES

DATE

TRAVELING WITH

WEATHER CONDITIONS

FROM / TO

DISTANCE

TRAVEL TIME

TRAFFIC LEVEL

LESS 1 2 3 4 5 MUCH

TRAVEL ROUTE

STOPS & MILESTONES	TIME OF ARRIVAL	HIGHLIGHTS & NOTES

DINING EXPERIENCES

BREAKFAST	LUNCH	DINNER	SNACKS

SLEEPOVER EXPERIENCES

DATE

TRAVELING WITH

WEATHER CONDITIONS

FROM / TO

DISTANCE

TRAVEL TIME

TRAFFIC LEVEL

LESS 1 2 3 4 5 MUCH

TRAVEL ROUTE

STOPS & MILESTONES	TIME OF ARRIVAL	HIGHLIGHTS & NOTES

DINING EXPERIENCES

BREAKFAST	LUNCH	DINNER	SNACKS

SLEEPOVER EXPERIENCES

	DATE
	TRAVELING WITH

WEATHER CONDITIONS

🌡 _____ ☀ ⛅ 🌧 ⛈ ❄
🚩 _____ ☐ ☐ ☐ ☐ ☐

	FROM / TO
	DISTANCE
	TRAVEL TIME

TRAFFIC LEVEL

LESS 1 — 2 — 3 — 4 — 5 MUCH

TRAVEL ROUTE

STOPS & MILESTONES	TIME OF ARRIVAL	HIGHLIGHTS & NOTES

DINING EXPERIENCES

BREAKFAST	LUNCH	DINNER	SNACKS

SLEEPOVER EXPERIENCES

	DATE
	TRAVELING WITH

WEATHER CONDITIONS

🌡	___	☀	⛅	🌧	⛈	❄
🚩	___	☐	☐	☐	☐	☐

	FROM / TO
	DISTANCE
	TRAVEL TIME

TRAFFIC LEVEL

LESS 1 ○ 2 ○ 3 ○ 4 ○ 5 ○ MUCH

TRAVEL ROUTE

STOPS & MILESTONES	TIME OF ARRIVAL	HIGHLIGHTS & NOTES

DINING EXPERIENCES

BREAKFAST	LUNCH	DINNER	SNACKS

SLEEPOVER EXPERIENCES

DATE	
TRAVELING WITH	

WEATHER CONDITIONS

🌡 _____ ☀ ⛅ 🌦 🌧 ❄
🌬 _____ ☐ ☐ ☐ ☐ ☐

FROM / TO	
DISTANCE	
TRAVEL TIME	

TRAFFIC LEVEL

LESS 1 2 3 4 5 MUCH
      ○ ○ ○ ○ ○

TRAVEL ROUTE

STOPS & MILESTONES	TIME OF ARRIVAL	HIGHLIGHTS & NOTES

DINING EXPERIENCES

BREAKFAST	LUNCH	DINNER	SNACKS

SLEEPOVER EXPERIENCES

DATE

TRAVELING WITH

WEATHER CONDITIONS

☀️ ⛅ 🌧️ ⛈️ ❄️
☐ ☐ ☐ ☐ ☐

FROM / TO

DISTANCE

TRAVEL TIME

TRAFFIC LEVEL

LESS 1 2 3 4 5 MUCH
     ○ ○ ○ ○ ○

TRAVEL ROUTE

STOPS & MILESTONES	TIME OF ARRIVAL	HIGHLIGHTS & NOTES

DINING EXPERIENCES

BREAKFAST	LUNCH	DINNER	SNACKS

SLEEPOVER EXPERIENCES

DATE
TRAVELING WITH

WEATHER CONDITIONS

FROM / TO
DISTANCE
TRAVEL TIME

TRAFFIC LEVEL

LESS 1 2 3 4 5 MUCH

TRAVEL ROUTE

STOPS & MILESTONES	TIME OF ARRIVAL	HIGHLIGHTS & NOTES

DINING EXPERIENCES

BREAKFAST	LUNCH	DINNER	SNACKS

SLEEPOVER EXPERIENCES

	DATE
	TRAVELING WITH

WEATHER CONDITIONS

🌡	___	☀	⛅	🌧	⛈	❄
🚩	___	☐	☐	☐	☐	☐

	FROM / TO
	DISTANCE
	TRAVEL TIME

TRAFFIC LEVEL

LESS 1 — 2 — 3 — 4 — 5 MUCH

TRAVEL ROUTE

STOPS & MILESTONES	TIME OF ARRIVAL	HIGHLIGHTS & NOTES

DINING EXPERIENCES

BREAKFAST	LUNCH	DINNER	SNACKS

SLEEPOVER EXPERIENCES

	DATE
	TRAVELING WITH

WEATHER CONDITIONS

🌡 _____ ☀ ☁ 🌧 ⛈ ❄
🌬 _____ ☐ ☐ ☐ ☐ ☐

	FROM / TO
	DISTANCE
	TRAVEL TIME

TRAFFIC LEVEL

LESS 1 — 2 — 3 — 4 — 5 MUCH

TRAVEL ROUTE

STOPS & MILESTONES	TIME OF ARRIVAL	HIGHLIGHTS & NOTES

DINING EXPERIENCES

BREAKFAST	LUNCH	DINNER	SNACKS

SLEEPOVER EXPERIENCES

DATE

TRAVELING WITH

WEATHER CONDITIONS

☀️ ⛅ 🌧️ ⛈️ ❄️
☐ ☐ ☐ ☐ ☐

FROM / TO

DISTANCE

TRAVEL TIME

TRAFFIC LEVEL

LESS 1 2 3 4 5 MUCH

TRAVEL ROUTE

STOPS & MILESTONES	TIME OF ARRIVAL	HIGHLIGHTS & NOTES

DINING EXPERIENCES

BREAKFAST	LUNCH	DINNER	SNACKS

SLEEPOVER EXPERIENCES

DATE

TRAVELING WITH

WEATHER CONDITIONS

FROM / TO

DISTANCE

TRAVEL TIME

TRAFFIC LEVEL

LESS 1 — 2 — 3 — 4 — 5 MUCH

TRAVEL ROUTE

STOPS & MILESTONES	TIME OF ARRIVAL	HIGHLIGHTS & NOTES

DINING EXPERIENCES

BREAKFAST	LUNCH	DINNER	SNACKS

SLEEPOVER EXPERIENCES

DATE

TRAVELING WITH

WEATHER CONDITIONS

FROM / TO

DISTANCE

TRAVEL TIME

TRAFFIC LEVEL

LESS 1 2 3 4 5 MUCH

TRAVEL ROUTE

STOPS & MILESTONES	TIME OF ARRIVAL	HIGHLIGHTS & NOTES

DINING EXPERIENCES

BREAKFAST	LUNCH	DINNER	SNACKS

SLEEPOVER EXPERIENCES

	DATE
	TRAVELING WITH

WEATHER CONDITIONS

🌡 _____ ☀ ⛅ 🌧 ⛈ ❄
🚩 _____ ☐ ☐ ☐ ☐ ☐

	FROM / TO
	DISTANCE
	TRAVEL TIME

TRAFFIC LEVEL

LESS 1 2 3 4 5 MUCH
      ○ ○ ○ ○ ○

TRAVEL ROUTE

STOPS & MILESTONES	TIME OF ARRIVAL	HIGHLIGHTS & NOTES

DINING EXPERIENCES

BREAKFAST	LUNCH	DINNER	SNACKS

SLEEPOVER EXPERIENCES

___
___
___

DATE

TRAVELING WITH

WEATHER CONDITIONS

FROM / TO

DISTANCE

TRAVEL TIME

TRAFFIC LEVEL

LESS 1 2 3 4 5 MUCH

TRAVEL ROUTE

STOPS & MILESTONES	TIME OF ARRIVAL	HIGHLIGHTS & NOTES

DINING EXPERIENCES

BREAKFAST	LUNCH	DINNER	SNACKS

SLEEPOVER EXPERIENCES

DATE

TRAVELING WITH

WEATHER CONDITIONS

FROM / TO
DISTANCE
TRAVEL TIME

TRAFFIC LEVEL

LESS 1 2 3 4 5 MUCH

TRAVEL ROUTE

STOPS & MILESTONES	TIME OF ARRIVAL	HIGHLIGHTS & NOTES

DINING EXPERIENCES

BREAKFAST	LUNCH	DINNER	SNACKS

SLEEPOVER EXPERIENCES

DATE	
TRAVELING WITH	

WEATHER CONDITIONS

🌡️ _____ ☀️ ⛅ 🌧️ ⛈️ ❄️
🎐 _____ ☐ ☐ ☐ ☐ ☐

FROM / TO	
DISTANCE	
TRAVEL TIME	

TRAFFIC LEVEL

LESS 1 — 2 — 3 — 4 — 5 MUCH

TRAVEL ROUTE

STOPS & MILESTONES	TIME OF ARRIVAL	HIGHLIGHTS & NOTES

DINING EXPERIENCES

BREAKFAST	LUNCH	DINNER	SNACKS

SLEEPOVER EXPERIENCES

DATE		WEATHER CONDITIONS

TRAVELING WITH

FROM / TO
DISTANCE
TRAVEL TIME

TRAFFIC LEVEL
LESS 1 2 3 4 5 MUCH

TRAVEL ROUTE

STOPS & MILESTONES	TIME OF ARRIVAL	HIGHLIGHTS & NOTES

DINING EXPERIENCES

BREAKFAST	LUNCH	DINNER	SNACKS

SLEEPOVER EXPERIENCES

DATE

TRAVELING WITH

WEATHER CONDITIONS

☀ ⛅ 🌧 ⛈ ❄
☐ ☐ ☐ ☐ ☐

FROM / TO

DISTANCE

TRAVEL TIME

TRAFFIC LEVEL

LESS 1 — 2 — 3 — 4 — 5 MUCH

TRAVEL ROUTE

STOPS & MILESTONES	TIME OF ARRIVAL	HIGHLIGHTS & NOTES

DINING EXPERIENCES

BREAKFAST	LUNCH	DINNER	SNACKS

SLEEPOVER EXPERIENCES

DATE

TRAVELING WITH

WEATHER CONDITIONS

FROM / TO

DISTANCE

TRAVEL TIME

TRAFFIC LEVEL

LESS 1 2 3 4 5 MUCH

TRAVEL ROUTE

STOPS & MILESTONES	TIME OF ARRIVAL	HIGHLIGHTS & NOTES

DINING EXPERIENCES

BREAKFAST	LUNCH	DINNER	SNACKS

SLEEPOVER EXPERIENCES

	DATE
	TRAVELING WITH

WEATHER CONDITIONS

🌡 ____ ☀ ⛅ 🌧 ⛈ ❄
🎐 ____ ☐ ☐ ☐ ☐ ☐

	FROM / TO
	DISTANCE
	TRAVEL TIME

TRAFFIC LEVEL

LESS 1 2 3 4 5 MUCH

TRAVEL ROUTE

STOPS & MILESTONES	TIME OF ARRIVAL	HIGHLIGHTS & NOTES

DINING EXPERIENCES

BREAKFAST	LUNCH	DINNER	SNACKS

SLEEPOVER EXPERIENCES

DATE

TRAVELING WITH

WEATHER CONDITIONS

FROM / TO

DISTANCE

TRAVEL TIME

TRAFFIC LEVEL

LESS 1 2 3 4 5 MUCH

TRAVEL ROUTE

STOPS & MILESTONES	TIME OF ARRIVAL	HIGHLIGHTS & NOTES

DINING EXPERIENCES

BREAKFAST	LUNCH	DINNER	SNACKS

SLEEPOVER EXPERIENCES

DATE		WEATHER CONDITIONS

TRAVELING WITH

FROM / TO
DISTANCE
TRAVEL TIME

TRAFFIC LEVEL

LESS 1 2 3 4 5 MUCH

TRAVEL ROUTE

STOPS & MILESTONES	TIME OF ARRIVAL	HIGHLIGHTS & NOTES

DINING EXPERIENCES

BREAKFAST	LUNCH	DINNER	SNACKS

SLEEPOVER EXPERIENCES

DATE	
TRAVELING WITH	

WEATHER CONDITIONS

🌡 _____ ☀ ⛅ 🌧 ⛈ ❄
🚩 _____ ☐ ☐ ☐ ☐ ☐

FROM / TO	
DISTANCE	
TRAVEL TIME	

TRAFFIC LEVEL

LESS 1 — 2 — 3 — 4 — 5 MUCH

TRAVEL ROUTE

STOPS & MILESTONES	TIME OF ARRIVAL	HIGHLIGHTS & NOTES

DINING EXPERIENCES

BREAKFAST	LUNCH	DINNER	SNACKS

SLEEPOVER EXPERIENCES

DATE

TRAVELING WITH

WEATHER CONDITIONS

FROM / TO

DISTANCE

TRAVEL TIME

TRAFFIC LEVEL

LESS 1 2 3 4 5 MUCH

TRAVEL ROUTE

STOPS & MILESTONES	TIME OF ARRIVAL	HIGHLIGHTS & NOTES

DINING EXPERIENCES

BREAKFAST	LUNCH	DINNER	SNACKS

SLEEPOVER EXPERIENCES

	DATE
	TRAVELING WITH

WEATHER CONDITIONS

🌡 _____ ☀️ ⛅ 🌧 ⛈ ❄️
🌬 _____ ☐ ☐ ☐ ☐ ☐

	FROM / TO
	DISTANCE
	TRAVEL TIME

TRAFFIC LEVEL

LESS 1 2 3 4 5 MUCH

TRAVEL ROUTE

STOPS & MILESTONES	TIME OF ARRIVAL	HIGHLIGHTS & NOTES

DINING EXPERIENCES

BREAKFAST	LUNCH	DINNER	SNACKS

SLEEPOVER EXPERIENCES

DATE

TRAVELING WITH

WEATHER CONDITIONS

FROM / TO

DISTANCE

TRAVEL TIME

TRAFFIC LEVEL

LESS 1 — 2 — 3 — 4 — 5 MUCH

TRAVEL ROUTE

STOPS & MILESTONES	TIME OF ARRIVAL	HIGHLIGHTS & NOTES

DINING EXPERIENCES

BREAKFAST	LUNCH	DINNER	SNACKS

SLEEPOVER EXPERIENCES

DATE	
TRAVELING WITH	

WEATHER CONDITIONS

🌡 _____ ☀ ⛅ 🌧 ⛈ ❄
💨 _____ ☐ ☐ ☐ ☐ ☐

FROM / TO	
DISTANCE	
TRAVEL TIME	

TRAFFIC LEVEL

LESS 1 — 2 — 3 — 4 — 5 MUCH

TRAVEL ROUTE

STOPS & MILESTONES	TIME OF ARRIVAL	HIGHLIGHTS & NOTES

DINING EXPERIENCES

BREAKFAST	LUNCH	DINNER	SNACKS

SLEEPOVER EXPERIENCES
